KINGDOM OF
THE CRYSTAL SKULL

LEVEL 3

Adapted by: Jane Revell
Based on the story by George Lucas and Jeff Nathanson
and the script by David Koepp

Fact Files written by: Fiona Beddall

Publisher: Jacquie Bloese

Editor: Fiona Beddall

Designer: Dawn Wilson

Picture research: Emma Bree

Photo credits:
Cover and inside images provided courtesy of Lucasfilm Ltd.
Pages 58 & 59: D. Delimont, R. Fried/Alamy; M. Jodice, E.
Herran/Corbis.
Pages 60 & 61: Visual Arts Library, B. Patterson/Alamy;
Bettmann/Corbis; Photodisc.

Published by Scholastic Ltd 2008

Mary Glasgow Magazines (Scholastic Ltd)
Euston House
24 Eversholt Street
London NW1 IDB

Printed in Singapore. Reprinted in 2009.

Contents

Page

DR INDIANA JONES (INDY)

Dr Indiana Jones is an adventurer and explorer – when he isn't teaching at Marshall College, an American university. He is very interested in history and travels around the world looking for important things from the past. He's always ready for an adventure, but he goes nowhere without his favourite hat and his whip.

MUTT WILLIAMS

Mutt rides a big motorbike. He likes to look cool, and always keeps a comb in his pocket. He's young, but he's strong and brave like Indy.

MARION RAVENWOOD

Marion and Indy fell in love when they were very young. Then they met again – twenty years ago – in a bar in Nepal. Soon Marion was caught up in Indy's adventures. Indy has left Marion twice before. Will he do it again?

HAROLD OXLEY (OX)

Ox is a brilliantly clever man who knows about a lot of things. He's a university teacher like Indy. They were once students together.

GEORGE MCHALE (MAC)

Mac is British. He and Indy are old friends. They were together on lots of adventures during World War Two. But which side is Mac on?

DR IRINA SPALKO

Dr Spalko is a Russian scientist who wants to control the world. She is clever, beautiful and dangerous. She isn't afraid of anyone or anything.

ANTONIN DOVCHENKO

Dovchenko is an officer in the Russian army, and Spalko's assistant. He's good in a fight but he doesn't think for himself.

PLACES

MARSHALL COLLEGE
Indiana Jones teaches at this college. It is in Connecticut, USA.

NAZCA, PERU
The famous 'Nazca lines' near Nazca are huge pictures made in the earth. You can see them only from the sky.

IQUITOS, PERU
Iquitos is in the heart of the Amazonian jungle, about 1,000 km northeast of the capital, Lima.

EL DORADO / AKATOR
El Dorado is the 'lost city' of the Amazon. People say that it was a city of gold built seven thousand years ago. But is it just a story or is it real?

HISTORY
The Cold War

The story of *Indiana Jones and the Kingdom of the Crystal Skull* takes place in 1957, during the Cold War.

At this time, Russia was part of the USSR (the Union of Soviet Socialist Republics) or Soviet Union, and was controlled by a Communist* government. The USSR and its leader, Joseph Stalin, were very powerful. After the end of the Second World War in 1945, they took control of Czechoslovakia, Hungary, Romania, Bulgaria and Poland. The USA and Western Europe were very afraid of Stalin, of the Soviet Union, and of communism.

People call this time the Cold War. There was no fighting between East and West, but there was a lot of fear and hate. The Cold War didn't end until the early 1990s.

Joseph McCarthy was a US politician. In the 1950s, he believed that the USA was full of communist spies. Many people were put in prison, although there was little or no proof that they were really spies. The FBI** checked everyone who worked for the government. Then they checked soldiers, teachers, writers ... everybody. They made life difficult for thousands of people. Often people didn't know why they were in trouble. Most of them weren't communists at all, but they lost their jobs anyway.

---

* *Communism* comes mainly from the ideas of Karl Marx. People do not own anything; everything belongs to the government. People are paid what they need, so a doctor and a cleaner might earn the same.

** The *FBI* (Federal Bureau of Investigation) leads the fight against criminal activity in the USA.

CHAPTER 1
'You will tell us'

Nevada, USA 1957

The line of green army vehicles drove along the empty road. There were jeeps, trucks and a weapons carrier. At the front was a green Ford. Signs everywhere said 'Private area', 'Do not enter' and 'No photography allowed'. The vehicles climbed up a hill. At the top was a huge gate, and next to it a small guard house. Three guards came out carrying guns. They waved to the driver to stop.

An officer got out of the Ford.

'Sorry, gentlemen, but this whole area is closed for twenty-four hours,' said one of the guards. 'They're testing some weapons.'

The officer walked towards the gate.

'This order is for everyone,' said the guard, 'including officers.'

The officer continued walking.

The guard realised something wasn't right. He reached for his gun. Suddenly three soldiers with guns jumped out of a truck and shot the three guards dead. More soldiers jumped down behind them. Some hid the guards' bodies in the guard house. Others attacked the lock on the gate.

The vehicles drove through the gate and stopped in front of a huge building with no windows. Next to the building was a railway line. Two soldiers jumped from a truck and hurried to the Ford. They opened the back and pulled a man to his feet. He was a big man in his fifties, with dirty clothes and several days' beard. His body was black and blue with injuries.

'Not him,' said the officer. 'Where's the other one?'

The soldiers reached into the back again and pulled a second man out. He looked even worse than the first.

Indiana Jones had been a prisoner for two days. He was working with Mac in Mexico when they were both grabbed in the middle of the night. Since then, they had been in a plane and several trucks. Their hands were tied tight and their eyes and mouths were covered. For the past few hours they had been in the back of a car.

He looked at Mac. His friend for years. It was amazing they could both stand up after their terrible journey. He looked at the soldiers. US Army! He couldn't understand what they wanted with him. Then he heard them speak ... in Russian.

'Russians!' whispered Mac. 'This won't be easy.'

'Not as easy as it used to be,' said Indy.

One of the soldiers picked up Indy's hat and put it on his head. Indy could see his bag and his whip too. But not his gun.

'You know this building, don't you?' the officer said to Indy.

'I'm telling you nothing,' Indy replied.

The officer hit Indy hard in the face. He fell to the ground. The Russian got ready to hit him again, but just then a car arrived.

'*Prasteete!*' shouted a woman's voice.

A tall, slim woman got out of the car. She was about thirty-five and had straight black hair. A sword hung at her side. The Russian let Indy go and stood to attention.

'Where did you find him, Dovchenko?' asked the woman.

'In Mexico,' Dovchenko said. 'He was searching for things in the earth.' He took Indy's bag and emptied it onto the ground. Several valuable pieces of art fell out and broke. They were centuries old.

'Oh no,' thought Indy. 'All those months of hard work.'

The woman smiled at Indy. 'I'm afraid Dovchenko doesn't understand history, Dr Jones,' she said. 'But allow me to introduce myself. I am Dr Irina Spalko. I am very good at what I do. I know things before anyone else. An what I do not know, I learn.' She knocked on Indy's head. 'I am going to learn what is in here, Dr Jones.'

Just then, the huge doors to the building opened. Inside, there were machine parts, suitcases, pieces of furniture, and boxes of all shapes and sizes. Thousands and thousands of boxes, as far as the eye could see.

The soldiers pushed Indy and Mac inside.

'This is where your government hides valuable things, yes?' said Spalko. 'We are looking for a box that is two metres by one metre by two hundred centimetres. It's highly magnetised. You know the one that I mean, don't you?'

'I have no idea what you're talking about,' said Indy.

'You will tell us,' said Spalko. Her voice was hard. She took her sword and pressed it against Indy's throat.

'Killing me won't help you,' said Indy.

'You're right,' she said. Two soldiers took Mac and threw him under one of the trucks. His head was under a wheel. Spalko shouted something in Russian and the truck began to move. She looked at Indy. 'I say once more, Dr Jones ... you will help us find that box.'

CHAPTER 2
'Find him!'

'OK, OK!' said Indy.

The truck stopped. Its wheel was centimetres from Mac's head.

Indy began to think quickly.

'The box is highly magnetised, right?' he said. 'So we've got to look for signs of a magnetic field.'

With the Russians and Mac behind him, he hurried down a line of boxes. Then another. Then another. He turned right and then left, another left, another right. And then he noticed that the locks on one pile of boxes were not quite straight.

Indy climbed up a pile of boxes. Dovchenko and two soldiers helped him to throw down box after box. Finally they found the one that they were looking for. It was made of metal. On the side it said: SWELL, N.M. 7-9-47. Indy smiled. He knew that meant Roswell, New Mexico*.

They carried the box down to the floor. Spalko began to open it. Inside was a metal body bag for something small. Spalko ordered a soldier to open the bag.

The Russians were all looking at the body bag when Indy attacked. He grabbed his whip from the soldier who was guarding him, and knocked him to the ground with his shoulder. Then, with his whip, he hit the gun that Mac's guard was holding. It shot the guard on the floor. Indy threw it to Mac and then grabbed the other guard's gun. In seconds, Indy and Mac were standing back to back, pointing their new weapons.

---

* Some people believe that a space vehicle from another world crashed at Roswell in 1947, and that the US Army tried to keep this fact a secret.

'Guns down!' shouted Indy, 'or Dr Spalko is dead.'

Dovchenko and his soldiers began to put down their weapons. Then something strange happened. Spalko smiled. Indy turned. Mac's gun was pointing at his head.

Mac! Indy couldn't believe it.

'Mac, why?' he said.

'I needed the money, mate,' said Mac.

Dovchenko stepped forward and pointed his gun at Indy's head. 'Drop the gun,' he said.

'OK, OK,' said Indy.

But he didn't drop the gun. He threw it into the air. It fell heavily onto the floor and bullets shot everywhere, hitting some of the soldiers. Indy climbed quickly to the top of the nearest pile of boxes. How could he escape? He began to jump from pile to pile, trying to avoid the soldiers' bullets.

The soldiers were getting closer. Indy caught one of the hanging lights with his whip. Holding on to the whip, he flew over the soldiers' heads. Then he dropped to the floor and ran. A jeep crashed into him and he was knocked onto the front of it. Driving the jeep was a very angry Dovchenko. With Indy in front of him, Dovchenko couldn't see. The jeep fell down a long line of steps and hit a wall.

Indy fell onto the floor. He could see a railway line. Dovchenko grabbed him and threw him onto a railway flat car. The Russian jumped on top of him and put his hands around Indy's neck, tighter and tighter. Indy's face began to turn blue. He could see that his foot was near a switch on the side of the flat car. He gave it a hard kick. The motor started with a loud noise and a lot of white fire. The flat car shot through a tunnel and out of the building.

'Follow the railway,' shouted Spalko to the soldiers in their vehicles. 'Find him and bring him to me.' She watched them drive off fast. Spalko wanted to kill Jones, but she needed him. He was like a dog: he chased something until he found it. And now she needed him to find something for her.

The flat car was travelling at more than 300 kilometres an hour and Indy and Dovchenko were holding on for their lives. The terrible speed was pulling the skin from their bodies. One second more and they would be dead. But suddenly the motor became quieter. The flat car slowed down, then stopped completely. Indy and Dovchenko stood up with difficulty. They tried to fight but they were like two men who had drunk too much. Finally Dovchenko dropped to the ground. Indy fell off the flat car like a big bag of potatoes. On his shaking legs he began to walk towards the hills.

CHAPTER 3
Just in time

The sun was going down when Indy saw it. He couldn't believe his eyes. A town.

A perfect American town, with perfect streets, perfect houses and gardens. It was strange that the town began so suddenly. It was very quiet too: not one car, not one person.

Then he saw an army jeep with three Russians in it.

He ran quickly behind one of the houses and knocked at the back door. No one answered, so he went in. He found himself in a perfect kitchen with a big white fridge.

'Anyone home?' he shouted.

He went into the living room. A family of four were sitting on a sofa in front of a small black and white TV. They took no interest in Indy. He picked up the phone. 'Hello?' he said. 'Russian spies are in your town! Hello?'

He stopped. The line was dead.

'Haven't you people got a phone that works?' he asked. 'What's wrong with this place?'

He walked over to the father and grabbed his arm. It came out of his shirt! It wasn't a real arm – it was plastic. The whole family was plastic.

He ran into the garden. And there was the sign: DOOM TOWN, US ARMY NEVADA TESTING AREA. DO NOT ENTER! Then he heard a recorded voice. *'Starting count down,'* it said. *'Thirty seconds.'*

'This isn't good at all,' he thought. He ran back into the house. *'Fifteen seconds and counting.'*

He threw open the fridge door and pulled everything onto the floor. Then he began to push himself inside. *'Five seconds and counting.'*

He tried pulling the door shut but his jacket was in the way.

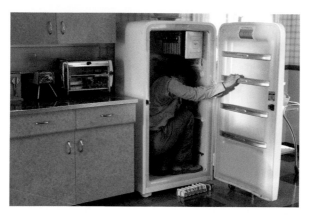

He tried again. The door closed as the voice was counting to one. Just in time.

There was a moment of silence and then the world turned completely white.

* * *

Far from the edge of town, a fridge fell into the soft ground. The door opened, and a shaken Indiana Jones came out. He watched the huge white cloud rise into the night sky. It looked like a skull.

* * *

Indy was checked by a doctor. Two men called Smith and Taylor were waiting for him outside the doctor's office. They were wearing dark suits and thin ties. 'FBI,' thought Indy.

'Your story seems to be true,' said Smith. 'But why were you in the Russian car at the start of all this?'

'I was taken prisoner in Mexico,' said Indy.

'With your good friend, George McHale,' said Smith.

'He used to be my friend,' said Indy. 'Before I knew that he was a Russian spy.'

'Are you sure *you're* not a communist?' asked Smith. 'You helped the Russians to break into a US Army building here in Nevada.'

'What was inside the metal box that they stole?' asked Indy.

'It's secret information,' said Smith.

Just then the door flew open and a large army general hurried in.

'Indy, I'm so glad that you're OK,' he said. 'Don't you know that fridges can be dangerous?!'

Indy smiled. He and General Robert Ross had been friends for more than ten years.

'Good to see you too, Bob,' he said.

Ross looked at Smith and Taylor. 'It's OK, boys,' he said. 'I know Dr Jones. He's one of us.'

'What's going on?' Indy asked Ross. 'Russians in the US? Who was that woman?'

'Describe her,' said Taylor.

'Tall, black hair, in her thirties,' said Indy. 'She had some kind of sword.'

General Ross looked amazed. 'Irina Spalko?' he asked.

Smith pulled out a photograph.

'Yes, that's her,' said Indy. 'What's the big deal?'

'She was Joseph Stalin's favourite scientist,' said Ross. 'She's interested in things which can help the Russian army. Strange things.'

'Don't say too much, General Ross,' said Smith. 'Dr Jones may be a spy.'

'Are you crazy?!' said Ross. 'Do you know all the wonderful things that Dr Jones has done for his country?'

'The FBI is watching you, Jones,' said Smith.

'Watching you very closely,' said Taylor.

CHAPTER 4
The boy on the bike

It was autumn in Connecticut. There were red, yellow and brown leaves everywhere. Indy was teaching his class at Marshall College, when Charles Stanforth, the college director, put his head around the door.

'May I have a moment please, Dr Jones?' he said.

Indy knew immediately that it meant trouble. He went out into the hall. 'What is it, Charlie?' he asked.

'FBI officers were here this morning,' said Stanforth. 'They searched your office and all your papers ...'

'And you let them?' Indy was very angry. 'They can't do that.'

'I'm afraid they *can* do that. American universities have to be very careful today. And people like McCarthy see communists in their soup!'

'So I'm losing my job?' Indy asked.

'Not exactly,' said Stanforth. 'We're giving you a very long holiday ... .'

'Why didn't you fight for me, Charlie?' asked Indy.

'I did,' said Stanforth. 'I said, "If he goes, I'll go too." I haven't got a job either.'

* * *

Later that day, Indy walked into the train station. He was on his way to New York. From there he planned to fly to London and look for a teaching job in Europe.

The train was already on the platform. Indy got on. He didn't see two men in dark suits get on too.

As the train began to move, Indy heard the noise of a motorbike. A young man on a Harley-Davidson was riding along the platform towards him. The rider was

dressed like Marlon Brando*: leather jacket, black boots, sunglasses and hair held up with styling cream.

'Hey, mister!' he shouted.

'You're nearly at the end of the platform, kid,' shouted Indy. 'If you've got something to say, say it fast.'

The kid pulled off his sunglasses. 'They're going to kill Harold Oxley!' he shouted. The motorbike stopped dead at the end of the platform. The train disappeared into a tunnel.

But Indy was on the platform, with his suitcase in his hand. He still didn't see the two men in dark suits.

* * *

Arnie's Café was crowded. They were lucky to have a table. The biker was showing Indy a photograph of himself with a serious-looking man in his early fifties.

'Yes, that's Ox,' said Indy. 'We haven't spoken for twenty years. So who are you?'

'Mutt Williams,' said the biker, shaking Indy's hand.

'Is Ox a relative of yours?' asked Indy.

* Marlon Brando was a famous American actor in the 1950s. He wore a leather jacket and rode a motorbike.

'He was like an uncle,' said Mutt. 'My dad died in the war, and Ox helped my mum.' He took a comb out of his pocket and combed his hair.

Indy looked at his watch. 'Kid, if you've got a story to tell, now's the time.'

Mutt didn't like following other people's orders, but he began his story. 'Mum got a letter from Ox six months ago. He was in Peru. He said he'd found a crystal skull. He said the skull had special powers. He was taking it to a place called Akator.'

Indy was suddenly interested. 'Akator? Are you sure?'

'Yeah. Why? What's Akator?' asked Mutt.

'If you believe the stories,' Indy whispered, 'it's the lost city of the Amazon. El Dorado.'

'I've heard of El Dorado,' said Mutt.

'Seven thousand years ago the gods asked the Ugha people to build a city of gold. That's the story, anyway. Since then, many people have searched for Akator ... and never come back. In 1546 a conquistador* named

* The conquistadors were Spanish soldiers who travelled across the Atlantic in the sixteenth century and took control of Mexico, Peru and other countries. See also Fact File, page 61.

Francesco de Orellana – the Golden Man – looked for Akator. He and his men disappeared.'

'So why would Ox want to take the crystal skull there?' asked Mutt.

'Well,' said Indy, 'some people say that a crystal skull was stolen from Akator, and that it has special powers. Control of those powers will go to the person who finds it and returns it. So is that the end of your story?'

'No,' said Mutt. 'My mum thought Ox was going crazy, so she went to Peru to find him. And now some guys have taken them both. These people think Ox has hidden the crystal skull somewhere. They will kill them if they don't say where it is. Mum said you'd help.'

'How does your mum know me?' asked Indy. 'What's her name?'

'Mary Williams.'

'There've been a lot of Mary Williams in my life, kid.'

Mutt was angry. 'Shut up, man. We're talking about my mum.'

'OK, OK,' said Indy. 'You don't have to get angry. How do you know that these people have got your mum?'

'She escaped and phoned me,' said Mutt. 'Then she sent me a letter from Ox.'

He gave Indy a piece of paper. It was covered in strange writing.

Two men in dark suits began to walk over to their table. Indy quickly hid the letter in his pocket.

'Come quietly, Dr Jones,' said one of the men. Indy could tell that he was Russian.

'And bring that letter with you. Or ...'

'Or what?' said Mutt. He had a knife in his hand.

'Or this,' said the Russian. He opened his jacket. The gun was pointing at Indy's head.

CHAPTER 5
Indy plays football

'On your feet. Outside,' the first Russian said.

The second Russian took Mutt's knife. 'Now!' he whispered.

Indy was angry with himself. He hadn't noticed the men. In the old days he used to be more careful.

Indy and Mutt got up. They walked between the two Russians through the crowded café. In front of them a college student was talking to a girl.

'Hit Joe College in the face, Mutt,' Indy whispered. 'Not too hard.'

'Gladly,' said Mutt with a smile. He hit him as he passed, and the student fell to the floor. The girl screamed and several people shouted. Then a general fight started, with everybody hitting everybody else.

'Come on!' Indy said. He threw his suitcase at the Russians and began to move towards the door. Mutt grabbed his knife and followed him to his motorbike.

'Your mum didn't escape, kid,' Indy said. 'They wanted her to send that letter. Now they want me to tell them what it means.'

'Get on!' shouted Mutt. 'Time to go!'

Indy got on. 'Are you sure you're old enough to ride this bike?' he said.

'Are you sure you're *young* enough?' replied Mutt.

As Mutt was driving through the heavy traffic, a car drove up next to them. Two pairs of arms came through the back windows and grabbed Indy. They lifted him completely off the bike and into the car. Indy hit one man on the nose and kicked the other in the face. Then he got out of the window and jumped back onto the bike.

Ahead of them, another car tried to stop the bike. Mutt took a fast turn to the right – up the steps of the town library and into the building. Students ran everywhere. Books and magazines flew into the air. Mutt laughed. He was enjoying himself so much that he didn't see the wall in front of him. The bike fell on its side.

Mutt was up again in seconds, but Indy was slower. 'I'm driving,' he shouted.

'No way!' laughed Mutt. He took his comb out and combed his hair.

A student came up. 'Uh, Dr Jones,' he said, 'I've just got a question ...'

'Bad time,' said Indy.

The bike shot through the doors into the street. Another Russian car! Mutt turned the bike around quickly.

There was a game on at the college football ground. Mutt drove straight onto the playing field, chased by the Russian car. One of the players threw the ball. Indy reached out and caught it just as the Harley flew through the goal. The crowd got to its feet. Indy turned and threw the ball hard at the head of the driver of the car. The car crashed into a wall.

Indy and Mutt rode to Indy's house at the college.

'They're sure to look for us here!' said Mutt.

'Yes, so we don't have much time,' said Indy. He found the book that he was looking for and compared the writing in it with the strange writing in Oxley's letter.

'I thought so,' he said at last. 'Koihoma. A very old South American language.'

'Do you speak it?'

'Speak it? Ha! No one does,' said Indy. 'But I can understand it.' He began to write notes.

Mutt watched him. Then he said, 'You know, for an old guy, you're not bad in a fight.'

'Thanks,' said Indy. 'This is what Oxley's letter says.' He showed Mutt his notes. *Follow the lines in the earth that only gods can read. Follow them to Orellana's bed, guarded by the living dead.*

'Orellana was the guy who went looking for El Dorado, right?' said Mutt.

'Yes. But what does Oxley mean?' Indy stopped and smiled. 'Of course! He means the Nazca lines.'

He jumped up and pulled down a large book. He opened it for Mutt. There were two pages of photographs of huge animal pictures taken from the air.

'The Nazca lines were made as early as 200 BC*,' Indy said. 'You can only see them from the air. Do you see? Only gods can read them because gods live in the sky. Oxley's telling us that the crystal skull is somewhere in Nazca, Peru.'

Indy pulled out his hat and his whip from a cupboard. 'Come on, Mutt,' he said. 'We're going to Peru!'

* *200 BC means two hundred years before the birth of Jesus Christ.*

CHAPTER 6
Skeleton attack

Mutt was beginning to wish that he had stayed at home. It was so hot in Nazca, and the food was always the same: rice and chicken every day. Indy was crazy. He told stories all the time about the Incas* and the sad history of South America. But they hadn't found his mum, or Oxley, or the crystal skull.

Mutt was in the square one afternoon when Indy arrived.

'I've found someone who remembers Ox,' he said. 'Ox came into town like a wild man two months ago. Nobody could calm him, so they took him to a hospital for mad people. It's on the edge of town. Come on.'

Indy walked fast. Mutt had to hurry to stay next to him.

'What language do the mountain people speak here?' asked Mutt. 'It's not Spanish, is it?'

'Quechua,' said Indy. 'The Incas used to speak it. I learnt it when I was quite young, from a man that I knew in Mexico. It's a long story. Things were a bit difficult with my parents at the time.'

'Things are a bit difficult with my mum too,' said Mutt. 'She didn't want me to leave school, but I did.'

'So you're working?'

'Yes, mending motorbikes. Anything wrong with that?'

'Not a thing, kid,' said Indy. 'And don't let anyone tell you anything different.' He stopped suddenly and turned.

'What is it?' asked Mutt.

'Probably nothing,' said Indy. 'It just felt like someone was watching us.'

* * *

* The Incas controlled a large part of South America before the Spanish conquistadors arrived. See also Fact File, page 61.

The hospital was in a very old building. A nurse answered the door.

'We're looking for an American named Harold Oxley,' explained Indy in Spanish.

'Some men came and took him away,' said the nurse. 'Men with guns.'

'Could you show us his room, please?'

She led them down a long, dark hall. Mutt walked slowly. Through small windows in the thick doors he could see men and women in dirty clothes. Some were crying. Some were screaming. Some were talking to themselves. Some were laughing madly. Some were silent.

A man suddenly put his hands through the window and grabbed Mutt's jacket. He pulled him against the door. Another pair of hands pulled Mutt free. It was Indy.

'Try to walk faster, Mutt,' he said.

The nurse unlocked one of the rooms. She pushed open the heavy door. They went inside. The walls were completely covered from top to bottom with drawings. Drawings of skulls. Strange-shaped skulls with huge eyes.

'Oh no!' said Mutt. 'Ox really was mad!'

There were words on the walls too, in lots of different languages. Indy was looking at them carefully. 'Every word means *return*,' he said. 'But return where?'

He got down on the floor and cleared away some earth. He found a drawing. Mutt helped him clear the rest.

'What is it?' asked Mutt.

'A grave,' said Indy. 'Ox told us to follow the lines to Orellana's bed. I think he meant his resting place ... his grave.'

'But you said Orellana and his soldiers disappeared in 1546,' said Mutt.

'Yes,' said Indy. 'It looks like Oxley found him.'

* * *

The moon shone down on Indy and Mutt as they reached the top of the hill. They went through a gate with a sign: MATAREMOS A LOS HUAQUEROS *We will kill grave robbers.*

'Lucky we're not grave robbers,' laughed Indy.

There were graves all around them. Mutt was frightened.

'Why did they put their dead up here?' he whispered.

'To be near their gods: the sun and the sky,' said Indy.

Many of the graves were open. Skeletons lay everywhere. Mutt thought he saw something move.

'What was that?' he said.

'Nothing,' said Indy, 'just ...'

Suddenly two bodies fell on them from the trees and attacked them. They looked like skeletons.

Indy fought with his whip. Mutt fought with his knife. But their attackers continued fighting. Finally Indy pulled out his gun, and the 'skeletons' disappeared into the night.

'Who were those guys?' asked Mutt.

'Modern Nazca fighters,' said Indy. 'The 'living dead' that guard Orellana's bed.'

They found a high stone wall with skulls in it.

Footprints went towards and away from the wall. Just above the footprints was a skull.

Indy suddenly understood. He put his thumb and middle finger into the skull's eye holes and pulled. The stone wall opened. Behind it was a large black tunnel.

Mutt got down on his hands and knees and went into the tunnel. He came out again very quickly. His arms were covered in scorpions.

'Help! It got me!' shouted Mutt. 'I'm going to die!'

Indy helped knock the scorpions off Mutt's arms. 'It's OK. They're only scorpions,' he said.

'Only? Only?! Look at my arm!'

'How big was the scorpion that got you?' asked Indy.

'Huge.'

'Good.'

'Good?'

'Yeah, good. With scorpions, the bigger the better. It's the small ones that can kill you.'

CHAPTER 7
The skull

Indy went into the tunnel carrying a lamp. Mutt followed. They went down some stone steps. Down and down until they came to the entrance of a small room.

'Don't touch a thing,' said Indy. He passed the lamp across the ground. Again they saw footprints, going in and out of the room. The footprints ended at a low wall. Against the wall were several silvery bags. Indy got down and opened the nearest bag. Inside was the perfect body of a bearded conquistador.

'There are seven bags!' he said excitedly. 'It's them! Orellana and his men.'

Mutt looked at the conquistador in amazement. 'It looks like the body of someone who died yesterday!'

'Everything's perfect,' said Indy. 'Clothes, skin ...' He touched the silvery bag. 'This is what we saw in Nevada.'

Indy took a golden knife from the conquistador's hands. He looked at it carefully.

'Uh, I thought you said we weren't grave robbers,' said Mutt.

'I'm not planning to keep it,' said Indy. He turned to put it back and jumped. In seconds the conquistador had aged five hundred years.

'This bag is already open,' called Mutt from the other side of the room. Indy went to look. The conquistador's face shone with gold.

'The Golden Man,' Indy said. 'Francisco de Orellana himself.' He touched the golden face. 'Something's not right. The Spanish never used gold on the faces of their dead.' He pulled Orellana forward. Behind the body he found a second skull. He lifted it out. It was a crystal skull with huge eyes. It had an unusually long head shape – the same shape as the skulls in Oxley's drawings.

'I've never seen anything like this,' Indy said.

'Do you think Orellana stole it from Akator?' asked Mutt.

'Maybe,' said Indy. 'And Ox found it here.' He looked at the skull for a long time. It was impossible to look away. He began to feel very strange. Half asleep and half awake.

Suddenly Mutt shouted. The ground under him fell away. He grabbed Orellana's leg as he fell through the hole. He was hanging over the valley, which was hundreds of metres below. Indy threw himself on the ground and held the top of Orellana's body. He dropped the skull and it fell through the hole.

'The skull!' he shouted.

'Got it!' shouted Mutt.

Indy pulled and pulled. Finally Mutt was there beside him, and Orellana's skeleton fell through the hole into the night. Indy grabbed the skull from Mutt and they raced back the way that they had come.

* * *

They came out of the stone wall. And there was Mac. Beside him was Antonin Dovchenko.

'Hello, mate,' said Mac.

Dovchenko lifted his gun and brought it down hard on Indy's head. Then he did the same to Mutt. Both men fell to the ground.

Dovchenko picked up a large stone to hit Indy's head with.

'No,' shouted Mac. 'She wants him alive.'

CHAPTER 8
A mind weapon

Indy was extremely thirsty. His hands were tied. He opened his eyes and saw that he was in a large tent. The air was hot and heavy. Jungle air. Amazonian jungle air.

A hand put a glass against his mouth. Water. He drank and immediately coughed. It tasted terrible.

He heard Mac's laugh and looked up. His old friend was sitting in a chair opposite him.

'I've saved your life three times now,' Mac said. 'The first time that we met. Then in Jakarta. And now in Nazca.'

'Tell me something, Mac,' said Indy. 'How many names did you give the Reds* after the war? How many good men died because of you? As soon as my hands are free, I'm going to break your nose.'

'I'm not a communist, Indy.' Mac looked at a tape recorder on a small table. 'I'm only interested in their money. I need you to understand that. *Just like in Berlin.*'

The tent opened and Irina Spalko walked in.

'I'm very glad that we didn't kill you in Nevada, Dr Jones,' Spalko said. 'You are going to be so useful.'

'Always happy to help,' said Indy.

'America has done terrible things to the Russian people,' Spalko said. 'But now, Dr Jones, we have weapons that America will fear. The skull is a mind weapon. It was Stalin's dream to fight wars in this way.'

'So Oxley hid it,' said Indy. 'He knew you wanted it.'

Spalko sat down and poured herself a drink.

'You think I'm mad, Dr Jones,' she said. 'I'm not. The skull is very, very special. It was stolen from Akator in

* During the Cold War, people sometimes called communists 'Reds'.

the fifteenth century. Control of its powers will go to the person who returns it.'

'I know the story,' said Indy. 'But what if Akator doesn't exist?'

'We think it does exist, Dr Jones,' she said. 'In fact, we're certain that Professor Oxley has been there.'

'Ox is here?' said Indy.

'Yes and no,' Spalko said. She smiled.

***

Outside the tent, Indy was amazed by the size of Spalko's army. There were twenty or thirty soldiers, jeeps, trucks, water vehicles and a huge vehicle with a large knife for destroying trees. A jungle destroyer.

And there was Oxley. With a beard and long, grey hair. He was dancing around one of the fires. His red eyes shone madly in the firelight.

'Ox, it's me – Indy,' Indy shouted. 'You remember me, don't you?'

Oxley stopped dancing.

'We went to university together. I'm Indy. Remember?'

Oxley started dancing again and talking to himself. Indy turned quickly to Spalko and Mac.

'What did you do to him?'

'Nothing,' said Mac. 'It was the skull.'

'He will lead us to Akator,' said Spalko. 'And you, Dr Jones, will help him remember the way.'

* * *

They took Indy into another tent and tied him to a chair. They put the crystal skull on the table in front of him.

'Professor Oxley looked at the skull for too long. He went mad,' said Spalko. 'I want you to go just mad enough to understand him.'

The eyes of the skull suddenly became very bright. Indy tried very hard not to look at them but it was impossible.

'There could be hundreds of skulls like this at Akator, perhaps thousands,' Spalko said. 'When we find them, we will know the secrets of our enemies. And we will control the mind of every person in the world.'

Indy's eyes were on the skull. 'Return ...' he said sleepily.

At the fire, Oxley suddenly stopped dancing and said, 'Return ...'

Blood began to come out of Indy's eyes and run down his face.

'That's enough!' shouted Mac. 'We'll never find Akator if he dies.'

One of the soldiers quickly covered the skull.

'Untie him,' said Spalko. 'Hurry. We must bring Jones and Oxley together.'

Dovchenko untied Indy's right arm. Immediately it flew into Mac's face with a *bang*.

'You've broken my nose!' Mac whispered.

'I said I would,' replied Indy.

CHAPTER 9
Mutt's mum

As Spalko and Mac brought Indy out of the tent, two soldiers pulled Mutt out of another tent.

'You OK, kid?' Indy called out.

Spalko took her sword and pointed it at Mutt.

'Wait, don't!' Mutt said. He pulled his comb from the back pocket of his jeans. He carefully combed his hair. 'OK, ready.' He looked at Indy. 'Don't tell these Reds a thing.'

'OK, kid,' said Indy. 'You're a brave guy.'

'In that case,' said Spalko, 'perhaps we can try something different.'

She shouted to her soldiers, '*Privedite zhenshchinu!*'

The soldiers began to pull someone out of a tent. A woman's voice shouted, 'Take your hands off me, you animals!'

Indy's heart stopped. He knew that voice. Even though he hadn't seen its owner for twenty years.

She was fighting and kicking. Her clothes were untidy and her black hair was everywhere. But she was still brave and beautiful. The same woman that he had fallen in love with – and left – twice.

'Marion!' he said.

She stopped fighting and looked at him. 'So you're here at last, Jones,' she said.

'Mum!' Mutt said.

Marion turned to Mutt, surprised. 'What are you doing here?' she asked.

Indy looked at Mutt, then Marion, then Mutt again.

'*Mum*? Marion is your mother?'

Marion turned to him. 'Do you have a problem with that, Jones?'

'I just ... I never ... I didn't think you'd ...'

'Didn't think I'd what? Have a life after you left me? Well, think again!'

Spalko pointed her sword at Marion's eye. 'Perhaps you will help us now, Dr Jones,' she said.

* * *

Oxley was sitting by the fire outside. Spalko and Indy joined him.

'Henry Jones!' said Oxley.

'That's right, Ox. It's me – Henry. Also known as Indy. Now, listen, I need you to tell me something. How do you get to Akator?'

'Through eyes that last I saw in tears ...'

'Ox! These people are going to kill Marion. You've got to tell me.'

'Three times it drops ...'

'How do we find Akator, Ox?' Indy asked again. He noticed that Oxley's hand was moving. 'Somebody get me a pen and paper,' he said.

He put the pen in Oxley's hand and held the paper under it. Oxley's hand began to draw. He drew lines, a pair of closed eyes, the sun moving across the sky, then a snake, and finally another line.

'He thinks in signs,' said Spalko. 'What do they mean?'

'Those lines usually mean water,' said Indy. 'Closed eyes mean sleep. A moving sun means time. And the last line is the edge of the world, but it often means *big* or *great*.' He looked at the signs in deep thought.

'The water sleeps ... until the great snake ...' He suddenly sat up straight. 'I get it! Ox is telling us the way to Akator,' he said. 'We need a map!'

* * *

The map was laid out on a table. Indy was moving his finger across it. Spalko, Mac, Marion, Mutt and Dovchenko were watching him.

'The great snake must be the Amazon,' he said. 'But what about *sleeps*?' He looked at Spalko. 'Where are we?'

'Iquitos.'

Indy looked at the map again. He read the names of all the rivers. 'Yes!' he shouted. 'What river sleeps?'

Spalko looked carefully at the map. 'The Sono River,' she said. '*Sono* is Portuguese for *sleep*.'

'Yes! Exactly!' said Indy. 'Ox is telling us to go to the place where the Sono joins the Amazon.'

While everyone was looking at the map, Mutt moved to the end of the table. He put his hands under it. Spalko and Dovchenko's faces were close to the map at the other end. Suddenly Mutt pulled up as hard as he could. The table crashed into the two Russians.

'Run!' he shouted.

CHAPTER 10
Ox brings help

Indy, Mutt, Marion and Oxley stayed close to the slow-moving green river and ran.

Marion was frightened. Indy had told her terrible stories about the Amazon. And now here they were. They were running for their lives, just like in the old days.

They finally stopped behind some trees near the river. It was getting dark and the moon was rising. They stood very quietly for a long time. A group of Russian soldiers ran past them on the beach.

Suddenly Marion and Indy felt the ground go soft under their feet. Their legs disappeared into the sand.

'Don't move!' Indy shouted. 'Just stay calm.'

Marion watched the sand rise to her stomach. 'OK, OK. I'm calm. I'm calm.'

The sand now came up to their necks.

'I'll find something to pull you out,' said Mutt. He ran off into the jungle.

'We need help, Oxley,' said Indy. Oxley went off.

Marion looked at Indy. They were going to die in the sand. It was now or never.

'About Mutt, Indy,' she began. 'He's ...'

'A good kid. I know.'

'Indy ...'

'Some kids do better if they leave school.'

'Indy, his name is Henry.'

'Henry? Bad choice. How could you call him that?'

'Because he's your son, Indy. Henry Jones the third.'

Indy's mouth fell open. 'Why didn't you make him finish school?' he shouted.

Suddenly something long and heavy crashed down

between them in the dark. Mutt was holding the other end. 'Grab it!' he said. 'I'll pull you out!'

Marion grabbed it first and was soon out of the sand. Then Indy put his hands around it. It was round and cold.

He took his hands away and screamed. 'Are you crazy?'

'Just grab it, Indy,' Marion said.

'It's a SNAKE! And it's BIG! Go and find something else!'

'Hey, this place isn't a department store,' said Mutt. 'What's wrong with you? I thought you weren't afraid of anything.'

'Just snakes,' said Marion.

'Come on, man. Grab it,' said Mutt.

Indy closed his eyes and held onto the snake. Mutt pulled and pulled and Indy was soon lying safely on hard ground.

Marion looked up to see two pairs of shiny black boots. Two Russian soldiers. Behind them, Oxley stood between Spalko and Mac.

'I brought help,' said Oxley.

* * *

The journey along the Sono River was extremely difficult, but the huge jungle destroyer could open roads where there were none. It led a long line of trucks, jeeps and water vehicles. Spalko was riding in the back of the first truck, with Mac in the front seat and Oxley behind her, talking to himself. She wanted to prepare for Akator. She took the skull out of its bag and looked at it for a long time. Nothing happened. She moved her head closer and took it between her hands. Still nothing.

'It hasn't really got special powers,' said Mac. 'It's all a big lie.'

Spalko put the skull back in its bag and sat next to Mac.

'You don't think that it's possible to read other people's minds?' said Spalko.

'OK, so what am I thinking right now?' Mac asked.

Spalko looked at him. Suddenly she put her hand behind his neck and pulled him close to her.

'The answer to your question is: *If I need to.*'

Mac went white.

'You wanted to know if I plan to cut your throat, didn't you?' she said.

* * *

Mutt couldn't believe it. 'Please tell me it's not true!' he shouted.

He was in the last truck with Indy, Marion and Dovchenko.

'My father was a pilot,' said Mutt. 'He wasn't just a ... school teacher!'

'I'm sorry, love,' said Marion. 'Colin was a good man, but he wasn't your father.'

'You married *Colin*?' shouted Indy. 'How *could* you?'

'You left me a week before our wedding,' said Marion.

'I didn't want to hurt you,' said Indy.

'Yeah? Well, guess what? You hurt me,' said Marion.

'Will you two stop it?' Mutt shouted.

'He's right,' said Indy. 'He doesn't want to listen to his mum and dad fighting.'

'You're not my dad, OK?' shouted Mutt.

'Sorry, kid, but I am,' said Indy. 'And I've got some news for you. You're going to finish school.'

'You said mending bikes was a good job,' said Mutt.

'I wasn't your father then,' said Indy. 'Why didn't you tell me?' he asked Marion.

'You disappeared,' she said.

'So why tell me now?'

'I *thought* we were dying.'

'Shut up!' shouted Dovchenko suddenly. 'I've had enough!' He went over to Marion to shut her up.

It was the moment that Indy was waiting for. He kicked the big Russian in the face with both feet. Dovchenko fell to the floor. Mutt pulled his knife from his boot and they cut themselves free.

'I'm sure you had plenty of women over the years,' said Marion, as Indy untied her.

'A few,' he said. 'But they weren't you.'

* * *

Indy came feet first into the front of the truck. He pushed out the driver and grabbed the wheel. Marion and Mutt moved forward and sat beside him.

'Take the wheel, Marion,' Indy said. He climbed back into the back of the truck. A few seconds later he returned with a huge gun. He put it on his shoulder and pointed it at the jungle destroyer.

'Cover your ears,' he said.

CHAPTER 11
Down, down, down

Irina Spalko saw something fly past her. It hit the jungle destroyer with a great *bang* and broke it into thousands of pieces. She looked behind her and saw the huge gun in the last truck.

'Jones!' she said angrily.

She grabbed a machine gun and began shooting at the truck.

'Drive close to the water vehicle, Marion!' Indy shouted. He jumped onto the vehicle and threw off two Russian soldiers. Marion and Mutt jumped on too. Indy drove fast, avoiding Spalko's bullets. Then Marion took the wheel. Indy threw himself into the first truck. He knocked the driver from behind the wheel and hit Mac in the face.

'You've broken my nose again!' cried Mac. 'You're crazy! I'm CIA*! I tried to tell you. "Like in Berlin," I said. Remember?'

As Indy drove over a fallen tree, the bag with the crystal

* The CIA (Central Intelligence Agency) gets information for the US government about people and governments outside the USA.

skull flew up into the air. Oxley caught it and held it tight. But a soldier grabbed it and threw it into Spalko's jeep.

'It was me who sent General Ross in Nevada,' said Mac. 'I stopped you going to prison.'

***

Spalko had the crystal skull. Now she wanted Indiana Jones. She pulled out her sword. She wanted to cut Jones' head off.

Suddenly something cut her across her stomach. Mutt Williams was standing in the water vehicle with a sword in his hand.

They began to fight across the two vehicles. Spalko was thrown across to the water vehicle. Mutt fell into the jeep and grabbed the bag with the skull. The water vehicle hit the back of the jeep and Spalko flew back into it. Mutt and Spalko fought again with their swords. Finally Spalko cut Mutt's face and pushed hard. As Mutt fell out of the jeep, Spalko caught the bag with her sword. Indy drove up quickly, and Mutt landed on his truck.

Unfortunately, they were just entering an area of thick forest. Mutt was caught by a tree. He found himself in the company of a group of monkeys. The monkeys used their arms to jump from tree to tree, above the vehicles below. And Mutt went with them! When he was above Spalko's jeep, Mutt let go and landed in the front seat. Several monkeys landed with him. They seemed to think that Mutt was their new leader. Mutt grabbed the bag and jumped into the back of Indy's truck.

'Not bad, kid,' said Indy.

* * *

Indy was driving fast to escape from Spalko, when suddenly he hit a fallen tree. The truck flew up in the air and came down on a huge pile of earth. Spalko's jeep hit the tree too and flew over Indy's truck. Spalko jumped out and pointed her gun at Indy. Then she screamed. A huge ant had bitten her hand. Suddenly there were thousands of ants everywhere.

'*Siafu* – army ants!' said Indy. 'We've hit their anthill. Everyone out!' Nobody disagreed.

Then Dovchenko arrived with lots of soldiers. He

jumped out of his truck and threw himself on Indy. Mutt and Mac ran to the water vehicle and jumped in. Oxley ran too, but he fell.

Dovchenko had his hands tightly around Indy's throat. Indy was turning blue and getting weaker. Hundreds of ants were running over both of them.

Then Oxley appeared and held the crystal skull over his head. The ants left Dovchenko and Indy and formed two rivers either side of them. Indy managed to get free. He stood up with difficulty. At that moment Dovchenko ran at him. Big mistake. Indy's shoulder crashed into the Russian's stomach, and Dovchenko was thrown into the air. He landed on his back in the middle of a river of ants. The ants immediately crowded into Dovchenko's mouth, ears and nose. He screamed. Indy had never heard a scream like it before. And then the ants carried Dovchenko slowly, very slowly, back to their anthill home. They were going to enjoy their meal.

Marion was still driving the water vehicle. She saw Indy racing to the river with Oxley on his back. She brought the vehicle close so they could get in. Then she drove to the edge of a huge rock, high above the river.

'Uh, are we going over the edge?' asked Indy unhappily.

'Yes,' she said. 'We are.'

Suddenly they were in the air. They went down and down until they hit the water. Water that was moving fast. Dangerously fast.

Suddenly Marion screamed.

'Waterfall!' shouted everyone together.

'Hold on!' said Marion.

'*Down ...*' said Oxley.

They fell and landed hard. Water poured into the vehicle.

Indy looked out. Spalko and her soldiers were running along the side of the river.

'Waterfall!' Marion screamed again.

'*Down ...*' said Oxley.

They fell again and landed even harder.

'*Three times it drops!*' said Marion. She pointed to a third waterfall, even bigger than the first two.

'*Down ...*' said Oxley.

Again they fell. When they hit the water this time, the vehicle turned upside down.

CHAPTER 12
The lost city

Five heads appeared out of the river. One by one, Indy and the others climbed onto dry land.

Indy went over to Marion and held her in his arms. Oxley took the crystal skull out of the bag and put it on the beach. It began to make a strange sound. The skull was pointing at the mountain behind them. As Indy looked, he saw a huge head on the mountainside. Water was pouring out of its left eye.

'Akator?' asked Mutt.

'We've found it,' Indy said.

'Through eyes that last I saw in tears,' Oxley said.

'We're going up there to return the skull,' said Indy.

'Without any climbing equipment?' asked Mutt. 'Are you crazy?'

'I have to do it,' said Indy. 'The skull asked me to.'

Mutt's eyes opened wide. 'It asked you to? A piece of dead rock?'

'What makes you think it's dead?' said Indy.

* * *

Indy and his friends had cuts, bites and all sorts of aches and pains. But when they looked up towards the eye with its waterfall, no one wanted to stay behind.

They climbed up slowly. Suddenly Marion fell. She screamed. Indy caught her and pulled her to him.

'Twice in one day,' she said.

'There'll be more,' he said, smiling.

Indy saw Oxley disappear into the eye. He threw himself into it too. The others followed. Behind the waterfall was a tunnel. Indy saw that the walls were covered with beautiful paintings.

The first one showed a group of people with their hands towards the sun.

'How old do you think these paintings are?' Mac asked.

'About seven thousand years,' said Indy. 'The Ugha artists were amazingly skilled.'

In the second painting, the people were looking at a tall, shining person. A 'god'. It was coming down from the sky.

A third painting showed several gods helping and teaching the Ugha.

The next painting showed the head of a god from the side. Indy looked at it carefully. It was the exact shape of the crystal skull.

In the next painting, thirteen gods were sitting in a circle.

And then there was a painting of war. The Ugha were fighting the conquistadors.

In the next painting, one of the thirteen gods had no head. The conquistadors were taking his skull away.

And in the final painting, the thirteen gods were dying.

'Why didn't the other twelve just leave?' asked Mutt.

'Maybe we'll find out,' said Indy.

They walked into a small round room. Thirteen skulls were at the top of the walls. Suddenly the skulls began to shake. Then they crashed to the floor.

* * *

Irina Spalko and her soldiers arrived at the water vehicle.

Spalko looked up at the huge eye. 'They've found Akator!' she said. She smiled. That meant that she had found Akator too.

* * *

The skulls in the walls became Ugha fighters. They had long hair, stone knives and a sort of whip with three heavy balls on the end. One of them caught Mutt with his whip. Indy rescued him and they all ran to the end of the tunnel. Oxley was already there, at the top of some steps.

And there was Akator below. It was inside a huge hole, with hills and clouds all around it. Trees were growing through the broken buildings. And in the centre was a huge pyramid.

They raced down the steps. More Ugha were waiting at the bottom. Two fighters attacked Indy. Mutt jumped on them. Then Marion shouted for help. A fighter was on her back, pulling out her hair. Indy waved his whip and threw the fighter into a stone wall. Mac was fighting three Ugha. More and more fighters were appearing.

'Harold! We're going to die!' shouted Indy.

Oxley took the skull out of the bag and held it above his head. Sunlight shined from its ears, nose, mouth and eyes. It made a strange noise. The fighters stopped and got down on their knees. Oxley moved towards the central pyramid. There were some stairs.

'*Up,*' he said. '*Up.*'

The stairs were steep and narrow, but they finally reached the flat top of the pyramid. There was a large square, filled with sand. Four tall, pointed stones were lying on their sides in the sand, forming a cross.

'*The key that opens the palace ...*' said Oxley.

Indy noticed that there was a small piece of wood pushed into a hole in each of the four walls. Some sand had come out of one of them. He picked up a huge stone and threw it down on the piece of wood. Sand poured from the hole. There was a strange sound. The tall stones were beginning to rise. Mac and Mutt helped to take out the other pieces of wood. The tall stones continued to rise.

Finally the four stones stood up straight, joining together to form one tall stone. The floor of the square opened a little. They could see that the tall stone continued a long way down. The floor opened further. If they stayed there they would soon have nothing to stand on.

There were stairs going round and down the stone. They jumped onto them. Then the stairs began to disappear, and they were hanging by their fingers.

CHAPTER 13
Indy has a bad feeling

Marion was the last to let go of the stairs. She screamed as she fell. Then she found herself in Indy's arms.

'Third time,' he said, smiling.

Indy didn't know where to leave the skull. He decided to explore one of the tunnels. The walls were covered with pictures. It got darker and darker as they moved away from the sunlight. But there was a green light.

They found a room full of beautiful bowls, plates and cups. Indy couldn't believe his eyes. He realised that these things came from many different places and many different times in history. Mac secretly put some in his pocket. His pockets were getting very full.

In the end wall of the room were two huge doors.

'How do we open them?' asked Mutt.

Indy looked around and saw a hole above the doors. He took the crystal skull from Oxley.

'Give me a lift,' he said to Mutt. He put his foot into Mutt's joined hands and Mutt pushed him into the air. Indy put the skull into the hole. The doors opened loudly onto a shining, brilliant room. It was so bright that Indy had to cover his eyes. In the middle was a large table. And on the table were thirteen seated skeletons. One of them had no skull.

Indy got the skull from the hole. They all began to move towards the skeletons when someone called out, 'Stop!'

It was Mac. He had a gun in his hand.

'Sorry, Indy,' he said, then shouted, *'Ya evo poimal.'*

Irina Spalko and three soldiers entered. Spalko took the skull from Indy.

'Speak to me now,' she said to it.

'It won't,' said Indy. 'You want gold and power. You're not a teacher. *They* were teachers. Oxley and I are teachers too. That's why it spoke to us.'

The crystal eyes began to shine. Spalko's eyes shone too. She walked towards the skeleton with no head.

Suddenly the skull flew onto the skeleton. It began to make strange sounds. The other skeletons made sounds too. Indy understood. They were having a conversation. Then the wall began to shake. The thirteen skeletons began to shake too. They changed into crystal and then skin began to form. They were coming to life.

'Tell me everything that you know,' Spalko said to the thirteen gods. 'I want it all. I want to know ...'

The thirteen turned to her. Their eyes began to shine ... with anger.

'I've got a bad feeling about this,' said Indy.

Suddenly the stone wall began to move round. In the centre of the floor, a cloudy shape appeared.

Indy and his friends raced for the door and into the tunnel, but Mac and the Russians stayed. The wall was moving round faster now, pulling watches, belts, guns and bullets towards it. Spalko took out her sword and it shot from her hands. It flew through one of the soldiers before hitting the wall. The soldier fell to the floor, dead.

'I can see! I can see it all!' said Spalko.

Mac ran from the room.

As two soldiers moved towards the door, they looked at one of the crystal gods. Blood ran down their faces and they fell to the floor in terrible pain.

Spalko tried to look away but she couldn't. The gods stood all around her. She began to talk wildly in their language. Blood poured from her eyes.

'I can see everything!' she screamed.

Suddenly her eyes caught fire. Smoke came from them and they went black. She fell to the floor.

One by one the crystal gods disappeared. The cloudy shape got bigger and bigger. It filled the room and then began to move into the tunnels.

CHAPTER 14
'Wait for me!'

Indy and his friends were almost at the central room. Everything was shaking so much that it was difficult to run. Suddenly water began pouring towards them. They tried another tunnel. The water was getting higher and higher.

Someone called Indy's name. He turned and saw Mac.

'Wait for me, mate,' Mac shouted. 'I'm on your side, remember?'

'You're joking!' Indy said angrily.

'You knew I was with you all the time, right?' said Mac.

'OK,' said Indy. 'Come on.'

They began to run, but the cloudy shape was coming nearer. Mac fell into the water.

'Can't move, mate,' he said. His head was just above the water. 'That thing's got me.'

The front of the cloudy shape was taking everything that he had stolen. It was pulling him back.

'Empty your pockets!' Indy shouted. 'It wants the metal.'

The shape was pulling Mac towards it. Indy grabbed his wet hands.

'It's no good,' said Mac. 'Let me go, Indy.'

Mac shook his hands free and immediately disappeared with a loud scream.

* * *

Indy ran to join the others at the bottom of the tall stone. There were no stairs. They couldn't escape.

Then they discovered a tunnel going up. There was daylight at the other end, but it was a long way off. They began to climb up. Halfway to the light, the rising water caught them. It threw them up and out of the tunnel. They fell on the grass above the city.

Akator was disappearing. The pyramid crashed down and water poured into the city. Soon there was a lake in the place where Akator had once stood.

* * *

It was getting dark and stars were appearing in the sky. No one spoke for several minutes.

Indy lay against a tree. He pulled his hat over his eyes and held out an arm. Marion moved into it and put her head on his shoulder.

'So we're just going to sit here?' said Mutt.

'Night falls quickly in the jungle,' said Indy. 'We can't climb down in the dark.'

Mutt got to his feet.

'Why don't you stay?' said Indy.

'I don't know, Dad,' said Mutt. 'Why didn't *you*?'

CHAPTER 15
Indy puts his hat on

Indy stood at the front of the church in a new suit. Marion wore a very simple dress.

Mutt was just behind his father. Harold Oxley sat at the front, close to General Robert Ross. Charles Stanforth and his wife were there too, with lots of other teachers and students from Marshall College.

Jones pulled Marion into his arms and kissed her on the mouth.

'Jones!' she whispered. 'You have to wait until *after* the wedding.'

Music began to play. Then the wind blew Indy's hat from where it was hanging. It flew up to the front of the church and landed on Mutt's boots. Mutt picked it up but, before he could put it on his head, a hand grabbed it.

Indy smiled and put the hat on his own head. Where it belonged.

THE END

Indiana Jones

THE MOVIES

The *Indiana Jones* success story began in 1981. Made by Steven Spielberg and George Lucas, the first film, *Raiders of the Lost Ark*, was an immediate hit. Two more films followed, and a fourth film was planned. But no one could agree on the best story to use. Fans had to wait almost twenty years before the fourth film reached their screens.

Indy – who is he?

Job: Indy teaches at Marshall College in Connecticut

Family: Indy's father, Henry Jones Sr., shares his son's love for history and adventure but he isn't always easy to get on with; he appears in the third *Indy* film

Favourite weapon: a whip, which Indy uses to swing on and to knock weapons out of his enemies' hands

Weakness: Indy is afraid of snakes – a fear which began when he fell into a pile of snakes as a teenager

Did you know?

- George Lucas chose the name Indiana for his adventurer because it was the name of his dog.

- Harrison Ford (Indy) was 64 when he made the fourth *Indiana Jones* film, but he still did most of his own stunts. Before filming, he exercised for three hours a day and ate very carefully.

- Russian actors play the parts of most of the Russian soldiers in the film, but Irina Spalko is played by Australian actress Cate Blanchett.

RAIDERS OF THE LOST ARK

When? 1936

Where? Nepal and Egypt

His assistant: Marion, his girlfriend from many years ago

His enemies: the Nazis and a French archaeologist called Dr René Belloq

His mission: to find a sacred box called the 'Ark of the Covenant'

> Have you seen any *Indiana Jones* films? Do you like them? Find out their names in your language.

INDIANA JONES AND THE TEMPLE OF DOOM

When? 1935

Where? India

His assistants: a singer called Willie and an eleven-year-old boy called Short Round

His enemy: Mola Ram, head of the 'Thuggee' – a group of people who use children as slaves

His mission: to find a sacred Sankara stone and return the missing children to their villages

INDIANA JONES AND THE LAST CRUSADE

When? 1938

Where? Italy, Germany, Turkey

His assistants: his father and Elsa (who is also working for his enemies)

His enemies: a rich American called Walter Donovan and the Nazis, who take his father prisoner

His mission: to find a sacred cup called the 'Holy Grail'

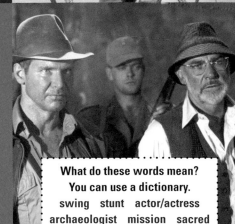

> What do these words mean? You can use a dictionary.
> swing   stunt   actor/actress
> archaeologist   mission   sacred
> slave

DIGGING INTO THE PAST

Archaeology is the subject that Dr Jones teaches at university. What is it?

Archaeology is the study of the past. Archaeologists look at the things that the people of the past have left behind – buildings, broken cups, money, and skeletons too. Often they have to dig away earth to reach these things.

Pompeii

Pompeii in southwest Italy used to be a busy Roman town. But in AD 79 it was completely destroyed by the volcano Vesuvius. For centuries it lay forgotten under metres of volcanic stone and ash.

It was discovered by chance in 1738 and archaeological work continues today. Pompeii's oil lamps, pots, furniture, beautiful houses and narrow streets show us what life in the Roman world was like.

A wall painting at Pompeii

58

The terracotta soldiers

In 1974, near Xian in China, there had been no rain for months. A group of men were trying to find water by digging a deep hole in the ground. One of them hit something hard – not a stone, but a terracotta statue of a soldier! After this, almost 8000 similar statues were found. They had been underground for more than 2000 years.

The statues are about 1.8 metres tall and carry swords and other weapons. There are real-size horses too. The 'soldiers' are guarding the grave of China's great leader, Shih Huang Ti (259–209 BC).

The Nazca lines

In 1927, archaeologist Mejía Xespe discovered 32 huge pictures cut into the dry earth at Nazca, Peru. There were birds, fish, monkeys, and other animals. The pictures are so big that you have to go 450 metres into the air to see them.

They were made between 200 BC and AD 700, but were the designers in some kind of flying machine or on the ground? And why were the pictures made? Did the Nazca people want their gods to see them? Did the pictures point the way to important places in the Nazca religion? It's still a mystery.

Terracotta soldiers

What might the archaeologists of the future find that people from our time have left behind? Will they understand these things, do you think?

One of the Nazca pictures

What do these words mean? You can use a dictionary.

dig   archaeology / archaeologist   volcano / volcanic   ash
statue   terracotta

INCAS, AZTECS &

Indy is very interested in the people who lived in South and Central America before the Europeans arrived. And it's easy to understand why.

The Aztecs

From 1427 to 1521, the Aztecs controlled a large part of Central America. Their capital city, Tenochtitlan, was where Mexico City is today. Religion was very important to the Aztecs, and they built huge temples to their many gods. Aztec temples were pyramid-shaped with a flat top, just like the pyramid at Akator in *Indiana Jones and the Kingdom of the Crystal Skull*.

All Aztec children went to school, but very few people learnt to read and write. The Aztecs had a kind of picture writing which was very colourful but very difficult to use.

Quetzalcoatl,
the Aztec sky god

What do these words mean? You can use a dictionary.
temple   knotted   rope   conqueror   civilisation

CONQUISTADORS

The Incas

From their capital city in Cuzco, Peru, the Incas controlled the area of present-day Peru, Bolivia, north Argentina, Chile, and Ecuador from 1438 to 1533.

The Incas had very good roads and amazing bridges across the valleys of the Andes mountains. They used knotted ropes called *quipu* to record information, but had no writing.

> Were there any great civilisations in your country in the past? What do you know about them?

The Conquistadors

In the sixteenth century, the Spanish conquistadors (Spanish for 'conquerors') sailed across the Atlantic Ocean to search for land and gold in the New World. The Aztecs and Incas were good fighters, but they couldn't win against the Spanish.

The conquistadors had powerful weapons and horses. In a few short years, they had destroyed these two great civilisations.

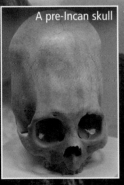

A pre-Incan skull

This strange-shaped skull, and others like it, were found in Paracas, Peru. Why is it such an unusual shape? No one can be sure.

Francisco Pizarro, conqueror of Peru (1532–1534)

El Dorado

The story of El Dorado (Spanish for 'the golden one') tells of the king of a South American people. He covered himself in gold and threw himself into a lake in the Andes mountains. Did he build a city called El Dorado too? Nobody really knows, but people have searched for it ever since.

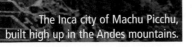

The Inca city of Machu Picchu, built high up in the Andes mountains.

CHAPTERS 1-5

Before you read

You can use your dictionary for these questions.

1 Complete the sentences with these words.

crystal   grab   kingdom   power   magnetic   tunnel

a) A thief ran up behind a tourist and tried to … her handbag.

b) After several years, the prisoners finally escaped through an underground … .

c) 'How did you stick those English words on your fridge door?' 'They're … !'

d) A country with a king or queen is called a … .

e) Be careful when you drink from those … glasses. They were very expensive.

f) The king had complete … over his people; if anyone disagreed with him, they were put in prison.

2 Which word is NOT connected with the **army**?

soldier   weapon   control   bullet

3 Match the words with the descriptions.

a) **whip**   i) a weapon which looks like a very long knife

b) **jeep**   ii) a long, thin piece of leather that is often used to make animals move

c) **magnetise** iii) to make a piece of metal stick to other metal things

d) **skull**   iv) a car without a roof that is often used by the army

e) **sword**   v) a place in a hot country with lots of trees growing close together

f) **jungle**   vi) the bones of the head

4 Look at 'People and places' and 'History' on pages 4–6. Who will help Indiana Jones in this story, do you think? Who will work against him?

After you read

5 Why is Indy in these different places?
   a) the back of a car   c) a train station
   b) a fridge   d) a café

6 Complete the sentences with the correct name.

   Mutt   Mac   Spalko   Indy   Oxley

   a) ... is interested in a metal box with a metal body bag inside.
   b) ... was helping the Russians in secret.
   c) ... loses his job after his adventure in Nevada.
   d) ... wants to help his mother.
   e) ... has written a letter in an old South American language.

7 What do you think?
   a) Who or what will Indy and Mutt find at Nazca?
   b) How will Mutt and Indy feel about each other at the end of the story?

CHAPTERS 6–10

Before you read

8 Are these sentences true or false? Correct the false sentences.
   a) A **scorpion** has got four legs.
   b) The bodies of dead people are sometimes put in **graves**.
   c) Your **mind** is in your feet.
   d) The top part of a **skeleton** is called the skull.
   e) Some **snakes** are dangerous.

After you read

9 Who says this? Who are they speaking to? About what?
   a) 'It's the small ones that can kill you.'
   b) 'I'm going to break your nose.'
   c) 'We think it does exist.'
   d) 'When we find them, we will know the secrets of our enemies.'
   e) 'He's your son.'
   f) 'They weren't you.'

10 What do you think? Is it possible to read another person's mind? Have you ever done it? Has anyone ever done it to you?!

CHAPTERS 11–15

Before you read

11 Match the two halves of the sentences.

   a) An **ant**   **i)** is a building which is wide at the bottom and pointed at the top.

   b) A **monkey**   **ii)** is often found where a river drops down suddenly.

   c) A **waterfall** **iii)** is an animal with four legs that lives in trees.

   d) A **pyramid**   **iv)** is a very small animal with six legs.

12 Guess the answers. Then read and check.

   a) Chapter 11 is called *Down, down, down*. What are they going to go down?

   b) Chapter 12 is called *The lost city*. Which of these things will they find in the city?

   i) more crystal skulls   **iii)** buildings made of gold

   ii) snakes   **iv)** people who want to fight them

   c) How will the story end for these people?

   i) Indy   **ii)** Spalko   **iii)** Mac   **iv)** Marion   **v)** Dovchenko

After you read

13 Number these sentences in the correct order.

   a) The water vehicle falls down three waterfalls.

   b) They climb to the top of the pyramid in Akator.

   c) Indy and his friends go into a tunnel behind a waterfall.

   d) They are attacked by Ugha fighters.

   e) They find a skeleton with no skull.

   f) The pyramid is destroyed.

   g) The vehicles hit an anthill in the jungle.

   h) Indy tries to help Mac.

14 What do you think?

   a) Do you like the way that the story ends? If you do, say why. If you don't, say how you would like it to end.

   b) Do you think Indy will have another adventure? If you do, can you think of some ideas for it?